Kind Words

Minna is a breath of fresh air! She is passionate, knowledgeable and by far a leader in her field. The service that Minna provided was above and beyond what I expected. I walked away from our sessions with confidence and direction. Minna took the time to understand me and my brand and what made me tick and somehow put it all together beautifully and easy for me to understand.

Cassie Calleya - Embrace Mind Body Wellbeing, Ocean Grove Geelong VIC, Australia

I truly thought that I knew enough about social media including Facebook. I met with Minna for her free 45-minute strategy session as I was curious and I was going through a phase of not enjoying posting on social media. I ended up booking two more social media strategy sessions! I highly recommend Minna. She helped me to fine-tune my core message and develop a content strategy that I am happy to implement. I've how have greater clarity and experience less stress and I will re-claim hours back each month. I highly recommend working with Minna from Social Media Tribe.

Nikki Smith - Nikki Smith Consulting, Ocean Grove Geelong VIC, Australia

I met with Minna from Social Media Tribe to discuss improving our Facebook page. Minna had so many great ideas of ways to improve our Facebook page and to increase the amount of traffic that are viewing our page. I highly recommend Minna from Social Media Tribe. Minna is professional and offers her customers a fantastic service, that is friendly, effective and produces results. I highly recommend Minna from Social Media Tribe.

Natarsha Sorensen - Tree Town Timber Flooring, Geelong VIC, Australia

I left the session feeling more inspired about my small business than in a long time. Thank you Minna. I can only highly recommend your services to anyone struggling with their marketing and wanting to raise their image and get clarity on differentiation from their competitors.

Paivi Bertucci - Bella B Photography, Melbourne VIC, Australia

My session with Minna was a vision shifting experience. She assisted me in seeing a more heart-centred method of interacting with my current and potential clients at a deeper level. Minna's energy and passion for helping entrepreneurs shined through as she walked me through the process of identifying my unique ideal client personas so that I can craft messages that serve and inform them best. Thank you so much Minna for your time and insights!

Beth Gayden - Author & Book Writing Coach, California, USA

Read more: www.socialmediatribe.com.au/testimonials/

In the Heart of Social Media Marketing

Heart centered, authentic marketing

By Minna Salmesvuo

Social Media Tribe

Printed in Australia.

ISBN: 978-0-6480553-0-3

Published by:

Social Media Tribe
PO Box 293
Drysdale VIC 3222
Australia

www.socialmediatribe.com.au

Reader Offer:

'In the Heart of Social Media Marketing'
Work Book available in March 2017

Order now through our website to receive your

FREE ebook

www.socialmediatribe.com.au/reader-offer/

Minna Salmesvuo

Owner and Founder of Social Media Tribe

Table of Contents

Acknowledgements

I'm eternally grateful for everyone who has been part of my writing journey and made publishing this book possible. I couldn't have done it without your patience, understanding, help, support and talent in editing, designing, reviewing and guiding the book's direction!

Especially a huge thank you to:

- My husband Chris and our two children who inspire me to be more, believe in me and support every crazy idea I decide to pursue without questioning
- Beth Gayden, my book writing coach, who provided me with the structure to work with and tools to make this book happen
- Mark Robert Waldman, whose book coaching session was invaluable in deciding the direction of the book
- Nikki Smith, my business coach, who helped sorting out my weekly schedule and make time for writing

- Mira Wannous, my accountability partner on this journey, who witnessed every step of the way and provided initial feedback on the book
- Richard Everist for excellent editing
- Lisa Hein from Evolution Design Agency for the stunning book cover design that I couldn't be happier with
- Dallas & John Heaton from Bluyonda Image Photography for professional photography for the book
- Susan Vukovic-Hiluta, my personal assistant, for all your work in the background
- My beautiful clients who are my constant inspiration for better and more effective strategies and solutions for social media marketing
- Friends and business networks for cheering me on along the way and sharing ideas to overcome obstacles in the writing process

My Big Why

Mission

To empower heart-centred entrepreneurs to make a difference by sharing their life-changing message with the world.

What I believe

I believe it is our responsibility to share the gifts we are given. We were given them for a reason. The bigger the game you play the more people you will help and the bigger the difference you will make in your own life and in the world!

You have a bigger mission and message within you and only by sharing it will you live your dreams – and help others too!

1. What is social media? Technology, people or a waste of time?

So, what is social media? When I asked this question during a recent business networking presentation, the first answer from the audience was 'it's a waste of time'. And yes, social media can easily become just that: a lot of wasted time and effort. This is the exact reason I am so passionate about helping small businesses realise the huge opportunity social media presents them when they approach the issue in a strategic way!

Another hurdle for businesses is often the unfamiliar, new technology that runs social media. There are hundreds of social media tools and platforms, and businesses often get discouraged by the technology. This can happen in two ways. Firstly, the technology may seem too daunting. It's hard to know where to begin. Or, the technology can dominate thinking when, actually, the most important starting point is to have a strategy and plan.

Social media is not about technology at all.

Social media is ultimately all about people and relationships! So when you start marketing on social media you need to begin with people. You must understand the people you would like to reach on social media, the people with whom you want to share your message. You must understand who they are, where they are, how they use social media, what they value, what they believe in, how you can make their day better thanks to your message and the services you provide. When you have this understanding you can start to build connections and relationships with your potential clients.

I think of social media as an ongoing networking event that takes place online. The only difference to a real life networking event is that you can attend it anytime it suits you without leaving home. Otherwise, the same rules for meeting and getting to know others, building relationships and finding clients apply.

It is important to remember the reason why people are on social media: they want to stay in touch with their networks. Their networks can comprise their family and/or friends and/or business connections. Building long-term relationships around shared values and interests is the way people connect and build trust in real life and the same is true for people using social media as well. Social media are not about technology. Social media are about people and, as with real life, building relationships is the recipe for success in social media marketing. People don't care what you know (or sell) until they know you care.

'People don't care how much you know until they know how much you care' - Theodore Roosevelt

'People don't care how much you know until they know how much you care'

- Theodore Roosevelt

SOCIAL MEDIA TRIBE

2. Why should small businesses care about social media?

2.1. Big reach with low costs

As a business owner, you know every marketing dollar counts.

Traditional marketing can be a drain on your funds and may not be a realistic option. Social media marketing, on the other hand, is pretty low-cost and gives you a direct line to current and prospective customers.

But there is a catch: What you save in dollars you'll invest in time. You have to be smart and efficient with the resources you have to achieve the results you need.

2.2. The opportunity to connect with anyone in the world

Internet and mobile technology allows us to communicate with practically anyone anywhere in the world. Many well-known people are just one tweet away - if you want to connect with them.

Local businesses now have the opportunity to grow their businesses into national or global businesses. Creating a global business and dealing with global clients can be easier than building a local business. You can work with clients remotely over Skype, through Google Hangouts, or with Zoom sessions wherever in the world your clients are.

The only question that remains is: how big are you ready to think?

2.3. It is never too late to begin!

Q: When is the best time to begin using social media for your business?

A: Five years ago.

Q: When is the second best time to begin using social media for your business?

A: Right now!

Yes, social media is getting busier and busier. And, yes, it will take time to build your brand and following. But the sooner you start the quicker you will be on your way!

2.4. There are hundreds of free social media tools

There are hundreds of free social media tools available to help you get your message out into the world. Small businesses have never before had so many opportunities to grow their business online.

However, it is important to understand that even though the tools are free, and there are many free strategies you can use to market your business, the more you are willing to invest in strategies that have been tested and proven to work the quicker you can achieve your goals.

For example, Facebook has made it clear that businesses have to 'pay to play' meaning that businesses have to pay for ads to increase the visibility of their Facebook posts. But there are still many cool ways to combine paid ads with your organic (unpaid) posts. This combination approach will deliver maximum results with minimum ongoing investment.

It all comes down to designing a strategy that best suits your business and marketing budget.

2.5. Your clients are on social media!

Even more important than the existence of free tools for your business is the fact that your clients are on social media! Whether you like it or not, that's why you need to be there too!

And if you thought that social media was only for young people, think again!

50+ years are the fastest growing social media user group and more than half of 50- to 60-year-olds currently use social media.

Some recent statistics (for those who love them):

- 72% of all internet users are now active on social media
- the most active are 18- to 29-year-olds with 89% usage
- 60% of 50- to 60-year-olds are using social media
- 43% of over 65-year-olds are using social media!!
- US citizens, Aussies and Brits spent the most time on Facebook (13-16% per hour)

- 71% access social media on their mobile devices (source: JeffBullas.com 2014)

Social media sites like Facebook have over one BILLION members worldwide, who spend an average of nine hours every week interacting with other members on these sites.

Not only do users of social media interact with each other, they also use social media sites for searching information on relevant topics. Did you know that YouTube is now the second largest search engine in the world after Google, and 4 billion videos are viewed on YouTube every day?

Whether you like it or not, your potential clients and customers are using social media and your business needs to go where they are!

In Australia, with a population of 24 million, there are 15 million Facebook users and five million LinkedIn users! This makes Facebook the must-have platform for businesses selling products and services to individual consumers. LinkedIn, on the other hand, is great for businesses selling products and services to businesses. (This is a general rule only.)

Other popular platforms that can work for your business include: Instagram, Twitter, Pinterest, Tumblr, YouTube and Google+. The right platforms for your particular business will depend on who your ideal clients and customers are, where they are online, what type of content you can provide, and so on. We will look into possible platforms in more detail later in this book.

If you thought of social media as a quickly passing fad with little relevance to small business, think again! The numbers speak for themselves. Your customers are on social media and if your business is not using social media to engage with them, the chances are your customers are interacting with your competitors instead.

2.6. The superpower of social media

So what makes social media so effective in spreading the word? Each platform is built for interaction: with sharing, liking, commenting, and newsfeeds. Most importantly, the connections between people build trust that can easily be transferred through recommendations to a third party or business.

Studies show that only 14% of people trust advertising, but 90% of people trust peer recommendations. Often we don't even need to know the people whose opinions we trust. A simple connection is all it takes: a mutual friend, a group, a shared location or interest. Just think about the power of the online reviews on TripAdvisor and eBay.

2.7. People are always connected to the grid

Would you have thought that 99% of Australians use the internet?

When you discover that 75% of people use the internet on their mobiles, the statistic starts to sound realistic!

Where do you go when you are looking for information? You Google it, right? So does everyone else!

These days almost everyone walks around with their smart phone within arm's reach. Most questions, enquiries and purchase decisions begin with Google, online reviews, online videos, or asking your network on social media. This is even true when the purchase is made offline.

Online and social media presence for businesses is no longer an option. It is the way of the world is today! Social media is here to stay and businesses need to adapt.

2.8. Five ways to use social media

Generating leads for your business is just one reason to use social media. The most popular ways to use social media include:

1. as a lead-generation tool
2. as a communications channel for customer service
3. building transparency, openness and building trust
4. gathering market research
5. positioning your business, or yourself, as an expert and building social influence

2.9. Most businesses are not using social media effectively

Another great reason for small businesses to quickly get up and running with their social media marketing is that many businesses are not using social media effectively.

We already know more than 72% of all internet users are active on social media and most buying decisions are made online, yet only 30% of small businesses have a social media presence and only 19% of these have a social media strategy! (Source: Sensis Social Media Report, 2015)

'Why do I need a social media marketing strategy?' you might ask. The answer is that without a strategy your social media campaign will lack direction and you are likely to spend money and effort and not get any results.

An effective social media strategy takes the guesswork and confusion out of daily social media marketing and gives clear actionable steps to follow.

If they do not have a strategy, businesses have no plan for their online branding, or how to find and connect with their ideal clients online, or what their goals are, or how to achieve them. So it is no surprise those without a strategy are not getting the best results from their social media presence. In fact, a lot of money is going straight into the bin!

In other words, since many businesses are not getting the best value out of their social media marketing efforts, there is a great opportunity to stand out in the marketplace – if your business takes a strategic approach through branding and messages focused on building trust and relationships with your ideal clients.

Many businesses dabble in social media a little bit but never set their mind to it and never really make it work. They are missing out on the opportunity, because they don't know what they don't know!

I just love the story of Joe DeFranco who went from a struggling gym owner to a world-renowned brand. Mastering social media marketing was an integral part of his success. His number one piece of advice to other business owners is 'Be a master of online marketing and social media'.

'It's amazing how many business owners and entrepreneurs still don't fully use the Internet and social media to their advantage. One of the quickest and most cost effective ways to get your name and company out into the marketplace is through the power of social media. A lot of people dabble in social media and content marketing, but not a whole lot actually take the time to master it and really discover its extraordinary power.

When I asked DeFranco how he was able to go from training athletes in a 500 square-foot storage closet and barely being able to pay the bills into the huge international brand that he has today, his answer was simple: "The power of the Internet and learning everything I could possibly learn on social media and content marketing."

Get serious about not just dabbling in content marketing and the power of social media, make it your personal business to be a master of it.'

(Entrepreneur -

http://www.entrepreneur.com/article/248506)

3. Common challenges with social media - and solutions

Do you have trouble promoting yourself and your business on social media even though you know your business depends on it? Do any of these common challenges resonate with you?

1. There are no results (leads, sales...)
2. Sites take too much time to update and manage
3. I don't know what to do with my page, or what to post
4. My content feels inauthentic and salesy
5. I'm not comfortable promoting myself or my business
6. The technology is daunting and changes often
7. It's difficult to stay consistent in managing social media during busy times
8. Nothing seems to be working or no-one responds to my posts
9. Does social media really work for my business?

If you said 'yes' to any of these statement, the good news is that the solution is easier than you may think! For challenges 1 – 8 all you need is an overall strategy that ensures all these aspects are addressed with solutions and action steps. Working with an experienced social media marketing strategist it is likely to take only a few hours to complete your initial strategy.

Your strategy should clarify:

- Your objectives and resources
- Your core message
- Your ideal client(s)
- Where on social media your ideal clients are
- How you can help them or make their day better
- What type of content can you easily create or access?

The challenge number 9 is more about mindset and the old saying explains this one pretty well: **'You only get out what you put in!'** It is simple as that! Social media marketing will work for you if you decide to make it work! It takes a little time to get started, but once you have your strategy, plans, tools and business processes set up, you can manage it all in an hour or two per week if that is all you can spend.

So instead of asking 'Does it work?', ask yourself: 'Am I prepared to make it work?'

4. Seven reasons why many businesses fail on social media

Without a strategy and plan your social media campaign will lack direction and you are likely to spend money and effort without results or, worse, get results that you did not expect. There are some famous social media campaigns – some by big brands - that went spectacularly wrong and had an effect that was completely opposite to the one intended.

On social media, 'one-size-fits-all' approach rarely fits! What works for someone else will not necessarily be the best approach for your business. You must have a deep and realistic understanding of your unique goals, strengths, challenges and resources.

The key to any social media marketing strategy and plan is that it will only work for your business if it is designed with your business in mind, and if it includes exactly what you need to achieve – nothing more – nothing less!

In our experience most social media marketing challenges lead back to one thing: something is missing in the marketing strategy!

The most common social media marketing mistakes usually fall into one of the following seven categories:

Mistake #1 – No strategy

This is the overarching, obvious mistake. No strategy means there is no direction, nothing that guides what you do in your online marketing on a daily or long-term basis. It is like travelling to another city for the first time without a map. How do you know which direction to go and when you have arrived?

This mistake often results in someone throwing around posts ('Oh no, I haven't posted anything for two weeks!') without linking them back to goals, core messages, and people with whom you want to connect. Sometimes people just hope something will stick! ('Phew, I've posted something now! It only took 30 minutes of panicking because I had no idea what to post!')

The symptoms of not having a strategy can look like this:
- managing social media takes too much time
- it is hard to find and create content
- there is confusion about what to focus on
- there is a lack of results

You wouldn't use a 'no-strategy' strategy for anything important in your life (planning a trip, your finances, a wedding!), so why would you use it in your marketing?

Mistake #2 – Not designed with your business in mind

Every business is essentially different because every business owner brings their unique goals, dreams, mission and message into their business. Your strategy needs to be equally unique. It needs to be the extension of your mission and message and to build a bridge to daily action steps. Your strategy needs to be authentic. Authentic is real, authentic can be felt, authentic is powerful, authentic works!

Mistake #3 – No sales funnel

Most of us know there is a certain 'process' to follow when you meet new people before you can ask them to lend money/join your email list/buy something. The same process needs to be followed when marketing on social media: you meet people, get to know them, build a relationship and then, and then, and only then, you ask (whatever you are asking)! In online marketing this process is called the marketing and sales funnel.

The symptoms of not having a sales funnel can look like this:

- Content is focused purely on sales
- Content is aimed at page likes or followers without any focus on how to achieve sales

Marketing needs to educate, add value, create goodwill and build relationships while solving problems.

People buy from people they know, like and trust – you need to build relationships first as part of your sales funnel. Once you have a process in place to attract leads, engage leads, nurture leads and convert leads, you can streamline, systemise and automate your online marketing funnel so it saves time, money and brings in leads while you are doing other things in your business!

Mistake #4 – I work with everyone or anyone

When you try to speak
to everyone,
you connect and build
trust with no-one!

SOCIAL MEDIA TRIBE
EMPOWERING YOU TO SHARE YOUR MESSAGE WITH THE WORLD

When you try to speak to everyone, you connect and build trust with no-one!

People look for messages and content that align with their values. They want brands they can believe in. Businesses need to communicate what they stand for and believe in order to build connection and trust with their customers.

'People don't buy what you do; they buy why you do it. And what you do simply proves what you believe.' – Simon Sinek

This mistake is always caused by lack of clarity around:
- who the ideal client is
- what your business' core message is
- what differentiates your business from other businesses in the field
- your own powerful message

To attract the right kind of tribe, you need to understand who your ideal client is. You must understand their problems, desires, beliefs and attitudes and how their daily life runs. When you narrow down your target audience, there will be many people who won't resonate with your message. Don't worry! Those who DO resonate with your message are the ones worth working with, because they are your ideal clients, the ones you can help the most and the ones who be most fun!

Mistake #5 – No plan to follow!

> You will never change your life until you change something you do daily.
>
> The secret of your success is found in your daily routine.

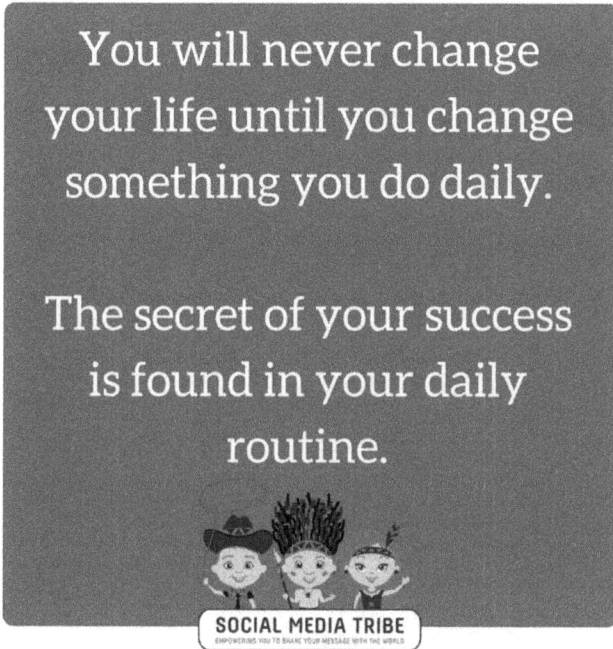

SOCIAL MEDIA TRIBE

'You will never change your life until you change something you do daily. The secret of your success is found in your daily routine.' – John C. Maxwell

Have a plan that connects your goals into daily action steps. Big goals make no sense if they are not broken down into doable steps that you can take daily, and track and measure.

Big goals without action steps are just ideas.

Mistake #6 – No action

"Insanity is doing the same thing over and over again and expecting different results."

~ Albert Einstein ~

SOCIAL MEDIA TRIBE
EMPOWERING YOU TO SHARE YOUR MESSAGE WITH THE WORLD

'Insanity is doing the same thing over and over again and expecting different results.' Albert Einstein

Sometimes, even when we have a strategy and plan, we don't do what we know we need to do. Not taking action is most often caused by one of these two things: old habits, or fear.

Old habits will keep us doing the same things unless you consciously choose to change them and keep repeating the new actions until they become the new habits. This is especially true if you are new to social media marketing. Starting something new requires developing new habits to keep your social media marketing consistent. Without business processes that support your new social media marketing plan, its average life expectancy is approximately the same as the life expectancy for new diets: 3 days! That is how long we can run things on willpower alone...

Even when your business is your passion, you don't love everything every day. Growing your business can be hard work. It often is. And then life happens!

A Day In The Life As An Entrepreneur

'No one ever got to the top of a mountain in one giant jump. Challenges can be overcome, and goals can be reached, but it can only happen one step at a time.' – Doe Zantamata

Have a plan you can follow daily and weekly, a plan that is taking you towards your goals and dreams one step at a time. A plan plus consistent action is what keeps you on track. Success is the result of daily steps taken consistently.

In summary:

- No Action = No Results!
- Same Action = Same Results!
- New Action = Different Results!

Mistake #7 – Not willing to grow and get outside your comfort zone

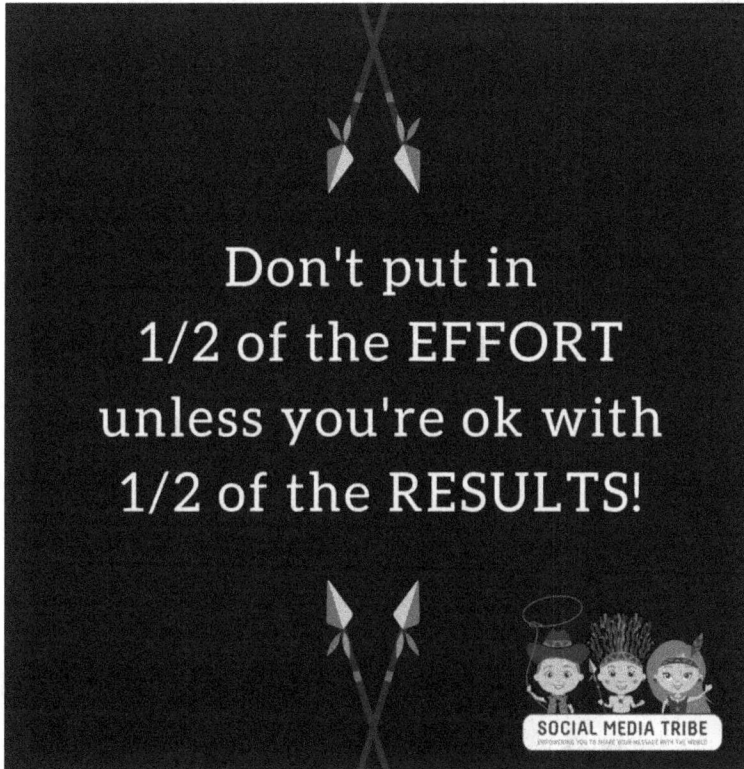

Don't put in
1/2 of the EFFORT
unless you're ok with
1/2 of the RESULTS!

SOCIAL MEDIA TRIBE

Fear can kill your dreams in thousands of ways. Humans naturally resist change. Our brains resist developing new habits because it takes energy. Playing a bigger game and changing what you have done so far is hard work, and growing means you will need to overcome fears, old emotions and beliefs to stay on track!

Doing different things means growing and getting outside your comfort zone, and it is not... well, comfortable!

All sorts of subconscious fear and emotions come up:

- we rationalise,

- we compromise,

- we procrastinate,

- we get overwhelmed,

- we get confused and tired,

- we have no time, not enough money, stuff happens...

All this is just FEAR wearing different costumes!

Doing anything new is guaranteed to take you outside your comfort zone. Growing and doing something new and scary is the only way to change outcomes. Whether the change starts within you, or the world around you forces you to change, change is inevitable. Staying the same is not an option in our fast-paced world. Accept it, get over it, get used to being uncomfortable, feel the fear and change anyway!

What this means to you, is that you must develop strategies not only for your tasks and actions, but also for your mindset - to ensure you take action on your plans every day.

When you grow, your business grows! And your business grows only to the extent that you grow... As is the case with everything else in life, you only get out what you put in!

5. What are the next steps in developing a strategy that works?

We have now covered the opportunities for small businesses out in the world of social media, the common challenges and strategy mistakes. It is time to pull everything together into a social media marketing action plan! Ready? Let's begin!

5.1. Understand what social media is and what it is not

Social media IS NOT about:

- technology, so don't just work with a tech-savvy kid who can set it up technology for you; technology is only where it all begins!
- a fad that is going to go away
- a magic bullet that can fix bad delivery and customer service; it only makes these issues more obvious!
- marketing only

People are not using social media just to receive your marketing messages. Their reason for being on social media is to connect with their family and friends and to receive news about things they care about. Your business needs to understand that not everyone wants to know about your product or service. The more focused your core message is and the more defined your target audience is the more likely it is that you will find people who want to know about your business or need your services.

Social media IS about:

- people, connections and building long-term relationships with other people and businesses; basically don't do anything you wouldn't do in a real world situation in front of real people
- creating visibility and credibility for your business subject to the terms and rules of the community
- direct access to your customers and clients anywhere in the world; just think of the possibilities!

Again just make sure you know your niche and that your niche is narrow enough!

5.2. Social media marketing mindset (and 'heart'set)

To tackle social media marketing, you must have the right mindset.

- Put yourself and your insecurities aside and change your perspective. It's not about you; it's about your clients!

- Make your messages about your clients. Show you know and understand your clients and what is going on in their lives.

- Focus on your message and the transformation your products and services can offer.

- Forget about the technology side of social media. You are still speaking to people.

- Understand that you connect with people on social media the same way you do in real life. It's no different. Don't change your voice when you write for social media. Be yourself. Be your authentic self just like you are when speaking with clients face to face or in a private message.

- Focus on your message and how you can help others help others through what you offer.

- Focus on helping others. This transforms you from a sales person to a helper. Think of ways you can help your potential clients, and how you can make their day better. If you understand their needs, your audience will feel that you really understand them, which will build a connection and trust.
- Focus on one ideal client type at a time. Think of the client persona you are posting to and then write your post like you were only writing to that one person
- Focus on the energy of your post and make sure it communicates your message. We can read between the lines how you felt at the time of posting. People respond to this energy more than anything.

5.3. The Four-step Formula for sharing your message with the world

1. Create a powerful and unique message that speaks your truth, and can be shared with your ideal clients.
2. Develop a social media marketing strategy to share your message effectively with the right people.
3. Use automated marketing systems and business processes to support you and leverage your time.
4. Ensure you are consistent in your marketing so
   → You can stand out in your market
   → You can connect and build trust with the right people
   → You can make offers and convert sales

Since social media is getting busier and busier, businesses need to be strategic in their approach and clear on their core message to get their voices heard. There are two reasons for this:

1. People browsing the internet make a decision on a business or website within 3 seconds of landing on a website or social media profile. That is all the time you

have to start building a relationship with your new prospects.

2. People are looking for more meaning in their purchase decisions. They want to work with businesses that align with their values and represent something they can believe in.

5.4 Everything is energy

On social media we communicate in writing and the reader can't see or hear us. It is easy to forget that our written words still carry an energy, a bit like non-verbal communication. Our written words have energy that can be felt. I call this concept the secret ingredient of online success.

Everything has energy and everything is energy. And your energy can be felt in everything you do. Have you ever seen someone walk into a room and immediately known what they are feeling, even though they are trying to hide it? Have you received a written message and known instantly that it was written in a hurry? This is what I'm talking about. We read the energy around us subconsciously without even realising we are doing it.

Everything is energy. Energy is everything. What matters is not WHAT you do, but HOW you do it!

This concept is useful when you tap into the power of your purpose and mission and consciously let this power fuel your social media marketing. Your purpose and mission has an irresistible heart-felt energy that can be felt in everything you do! But more about that a little bit later on....

6. How to design a winning social media marketing strategy

An effective social media strategy takes guesswork and confusion out of daily social media marketing and gives you clear actionable steps to follow.

6.1 Social Media Strategy 101

On a high-level your social media strategy will need to cover the following points:

- People: who and where are your people?
- Objective: what is your goal?
- Strategy: how will reach your objectives? Your Message? Your niche? What content will you offer? What makes you different from others?
- Technology: Tools and tactics? Marketing and the sales funnel?
- Results: ROI (Return On Investment) – you need to know what I and R are for you – what are your resources? How much time and money will you invest?

The more in detail you have around each of these points, the more in-depth your understanding of each step, the more clarity your strategy will have.

6.2 How we work

Our system for creating a winning social media marketing strategy starts with getting your business in alignment with your goals and mission, and designing a message, strategy and marketing system that is a perfect fit for your business. It includes:

1. Building your business and marketing from the inside out, starting from the purpose and core message that is hard-wired in you
2. Designing your strategy creatively to suit your unique message, goals, lifestyle, strengths, challenges and resources - not the other way around
3. Streamline, systemise and automate your online and social media marketing to create more freedom in your life to do more of those things that you love!

As a result, you will have more peace of mind and a feeling of balance because not only your social media strategy but your whole business will be a perfect extension of who you are. A strategy will really work for you when it is designed for you and not someone else!

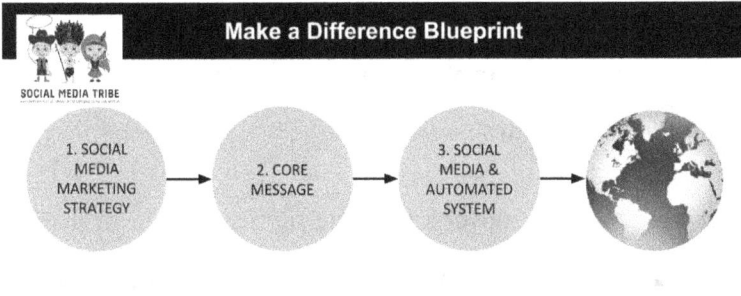

When working with clients, I use the following steps to design a customised social media marketing strategy that is right for your business:

1. Define your business and marketing goals – and where do you want to be. Goals, strengths, challenges, fun, natural talents, resources?

2. What is your core message and what are your core values? What makes you different from everyone else?

3. Who are your clients, who and where they are, what do they value and what problems can you solve for them?

4. What is your online branding personality and can you communicate your core message effectively?

5. What irresistible offers can be created by packaging your products and services?

6. What are the best social media channels for your type of business and target audience?

7. Connect the right content with the right people. Not just any content will work! Think content marketing with a big heart! Share your passion and core message, and delight your followers, with something that is easy to consume, shareable and engaging.

8. Develop strategies for capturing highly qualified leads.

9. Create promotions, competitions and campaigns throughout the year to keep the momentum going!

10. Develop an email marketing plan that builds relationships, offers value and converts customers.

11. Create an editorial calendar that shows the content that will be published, where it will be published, and when it will be published - to keep you on track daily.

12. Monitor and review results. What you don't measure you can't manage!

13. Plan for accountability and support to ensure you stay committed to your plan and achieve what you planned to do. There will be no positive results if the plan isn't implemented!

Online Marketing Strategy Blueprint

- 13. Accountability
- 1. Business, marketing goals
- 2. Core message
- 3. Ideal clients
- 4. Branding personality
- 5. Products and services
- 6. Best social media channels
- 7. Content marketing strategy
- 8. Lead capture strategies
- 9. Traffic creation strategies
- 10. Email marketing
- 11. Editorial calendar
- 12. Monitor and review results

SOCIAL MEDIA TRIBE

7. The power of your core message

It is vitally important to have a powerful message that differentiates your business from every other business.

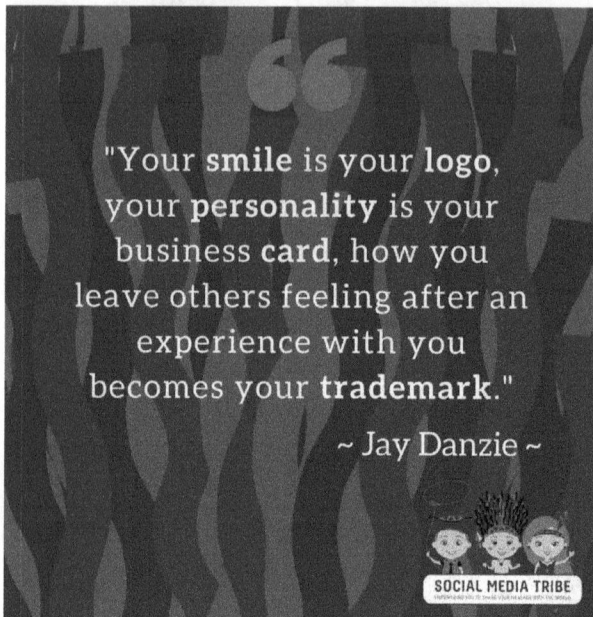

"Your **smile** is your **logo**, your **personality** is your business **card**, how you leave others feeling after an experience with you becomes your **trademark**."

~ Jay Danzie ~

SOCIAL MEDIA TRIBE

This is one of one of my favourite quotes. There is so much wisdom in it. Not only do you represent your brand wherever you go but your brand is based on your unique 'superpower' your big 'Why?' It is as unique as you are! There is nothing more magnetic than your authentic energy captured in your branding and message!

7.1. Why do you need a unique core message?

- If you try to speak to everyone, you speak to no-one. You must stand for something.
- Marketing these days has to educate, add value, create goodwill and build relationships while solving problems.
- People are looking for something that aligns with their values and something they can believe in. Businesses need to communicate what they stand for and believe in order to build a connection and trust with their followers.
- When you show your audience the true heart of your business, your core message, and what makes you different from other businesses offering similar services, you can start building relationships and trust with your ideal clients.
- Your ideal clients can instantly connect with your message, because they can see that you share their values and they can believe in what you stand for!

Benefits of a powerful core message:

- Your big 'Why?' becomes the guiding light for your daily business decisions and communications and reminds you why you do what you do and why what you do matters.

- Your big 'Why?' becomes more prominent in your branding, building trust and attracting those people you can help most and who you love working with.

- Your big 'Why?' becomes the theme for your content strategy and posting plan.

- Your big 'Why?' removes confusion about what to post and who to speak to, and your communication gains amazing clarity and power.

- Your big 'Why?' easily differentiates your business from others in your field

'People don't buy what you do; they buy why you do it. And what you do simply proves what you believe.'

— Simon Sinek

SOCIAL MEDIA TRIBE

'People don't buy what you do; they buy why you do it. And what you do simply proves what you believe.' – Simon Sinek

Your business already has a purpose, core values and beliefs, you just need to get clarity on what they are and start communicating them to your ideal clients so they too can see, hear and feel them in everything you do!

These days people are very savvy online consumers. They don't like being 'interrupted' and having marketing messages pushed down their throats. They are looking for meaning in their interactions with businesses. They are looking for something that aligns with their values and something they can believe in.

The essential steps in developing your core message are:

- What makes you different from everyone else? Consider your passions, values, goals, dreams and vision. Understand your truth (your big 'Why?') and uniqueness that makes your business different.

- Who are your clients and where are they? What do they value? What are their attitudes and daily lives like? What problems you can solve for them?

- What is your authentic online branding personality and how can you communicate your core message effectively? The key is to be authentic. People sense if something is not authentic.

- Find a tagline that captures in less than 10 words what you offer to whom and how you are different from others. This will convey your message in a succinct and powerful way that is prominent in your visual branding.

7.2. Discovering your unique core message

How do you help your ideal clients? I don't need to know the products and services you offer but I do need to know the underlying reason, the motive for why you do what you do. This is your core message. It is something that you believe about the world and people. Your life and business are this message!

You already know your core message. Deep down you know it. It is programmed into you and you will get flashes of inspiration when you know exactly what it is. You can find it in your heart. You will know when you have found it and you will know that it is the right one. Often our programming, beliefs and busy lives get in the way and you need to clear a space to get to this core truth. You need to stop thinking for a moment and start feeling and reflecting intuitively.

7.3 What is your business all about?

Every business is a problem solving business. It might solve a problem or two for you, but what I mean here is that it is ultimately about solving a problem for your client. Your core message needs to:

- Focus on your ideal clients and what they want and need.

- Speak directly to your ideal clients so they feel you understand them

- Describe your clients' problem and a desirable solution

In other words, your core message explains what you are trying to do, why and for whom.

7.4 - 10 steps to discovering your unique message

1. How does your product or service solve a problem? What is the experience it provides?
2. What is the reason your business exists?
3. What is the most important message for your business/the essence of your business?
4. What does your business stand for/believe in?
5. How are you different from others?
6. What are your core values?
7. What do your client testimonials mention most?
8. What do your clients worry about? Or are concerned about?
9. What do your clients want/need?
10. What are your clients' objections and what is behind their hesitation?

Look for general themes and words you have repeated in answering these questions. Use these words to describe your core message in a short statement that can be used in your tagline.

Don't be afraid to take a stand against what you don't stand for.

7.5 Test your core message tagline

Is your tagline:

- an outcome of your service that desirable for your ideal clients?
- powerful, passionate, showing your spirit?
- an authentic message – reflecting your core beliefs and values?
- something your clients can believe in

7.6 Share your message with the world!

Change in the world begins with you. It is in your purpose, your business' core message and it has the power to make a difference!

No matter how life-changing your message is, if you don't share it in an efficient way to the right people, your ability to make a difference is limited!

The next step is to take your unique core message and share it with your ideal clients. You can do this online or offline, in networking events, in social media, and when meeting potential clients. Your business' core message will quickly explain what you do in a powerful and meaningful way!

8. Finding your ideal clients

You actually get to choose who you work with! This might sound obvious, but for many business owners it is not. Especially when you are just starting out, it is easy to say you'll work with anyone, but once you have worked with 'anyone', you will never want to do it again!

Because 'anyone' includes people who create drama or don't pay their invoices, people who are negative and will never be happy with your services no matter what you do.

After you have worked with these people, it is safe to say, you will never want to work with them again! A big part of enjoying your work depends on choosing to work with those clients you love working with. And usually they are the ones you can help most too!

Your best clients are the ones who gain the biggest value from your services. The bigger the value, the happier they will be. The happier they are with your services, the more they rave about you to others and the more referrals will flow your way!

Not only does being selective make your work so much more enjoyable, but also it helps you to create your own little niche. If you focus your marketing to this narrow slice of the market it is much easier to define your branding and message, because you are not out there trying to please everyone.

In a marketing sense, it is essential to define your best clients, because this allows you to tailor your message to a specific group of people and show that you understand what they want. In doing so your prospects will feel a connection with you. Connection builds trust and trust builds business. When trying to speak to everyone, you speak to no-one.

So who are your ideal clients? Who are those people you would love to work with every day? Who are those people who you can help most?

Here's how to find out. Sometimes it is easier to say what you don't want and then turn it around into its exact opposite. Who can you help most? These are the happiest clients you can have, because you can add the most value to them.

Over time I have come up with this list to describe my ideal clients. I sometimes use it as a part of my promotions to ensure I connect with the right people. My ideal clients:

- understand and accept responsibility of their business and results,
- need training, strategy and ideas for marketing their business,
- are coachable, open, willing to learn and grow,
- want to considerably grow their business,
- are happy to invest and understand the need to invest time, energy and money into the growth of their business,
- are focused and committed to their goals,
- take action and get things done,
- face challenges head on and overcome them,
- communicate openly and honestly,
- pay invoices on time and in full,
- have a positive mental attitude,
- believe in themselves and their business,
- have a big vision and understand the growth process it requires,

- are ready to step outside their comfort zone and be uncomfortable,
- have positive expectations,
- understand the power of momentum,
- understand that everything is energy and we attract what we resonate.

8.1 Who are your ideal clients?

Describe your ideal client – your best client who loves what you do and who you love working with. Attempt to be and think like them in completing this!

1. Name
2. Gender
3. Age
4. Family and marital status
5. Education
6. Location
7. Where do they work
8. Financial situation
9. Annual spend with your business
10. Daily routine
11. Hobbies/habits
12. How do they use the web/devices/computers/social media
13. Their challenges, frustrations or pain points
14. Their goals and desires
15. What are their most pressing needs
16. Their attitudes
17. Their core values

18. Their hesitations, concerns and objections

How to use this ideal client description:

- Take your core message to the next level and write your posts directly to your ideal client. This helps your audience instantly connect with your message, because they can see that you understand them, their challenges and desires, and share their values.
- Target your blog and social media posts to a specific group of prospects by writing your posts like you were speaking to them one-on-one.
- Find your ideal clients online. When you know who they are, you need to have a presence on those platforms they use and you can join pages and groups online that align with their interests and values.
- Look for potential joint venture partners either off-line or online (Facebook pages and groups where you can network and follow conversations) who share the same ideal clients for joint and cross-promotions etc.

9. Consistent and engaging content marketing

'The only kind of marketing left is content marketing' – Seth Godin

After you have gained clarity on your superpower, core message and ideals clients of your business, it's time to start talking with them!

You content marketing strategy should include an editorial calendar that details your plans:

- what to post (the topics and content type, etc.)
- when to post (how often, the time and the day) and
- how to post (scheduled, automated from another social platform, or instant sharing)

The editorial calendar must be designed around your core message, ideal clients, their needs, and your online marketing funnel. The idea is to connect the right message with the right people by offering something of value. Your posts should educate and inspire, build trust and relationships. Your posts should make offers that solve problems for your prospects and make sales for you without having to be 'salesy' at all!

Most of all, content marketing needs to be engaging, delightful and fun! Your social media needs to stir some emotions every once in a while and make your followers feel something, whether that is happy, sad, amused, interested, intrigued, or surprised. Your best posts will those where you read your client's mind and say exactly what they are thinking!

Content marketing is often jeopardised because the availability (or non-availability!) of your time becomes an obstacle. Social media management can seem like a big hole where time disappears without a trace!

A great content marketing plan will give your content marketing a laser sharp focus, remove confusion about what to post, requires no additional work in creating your content and gives you a few easy steps to follow each week that produce your content effortlessly. It should cut through the millions of options available and simplify social media management into only what works for your business, industry, lifestyle, goals, audience, strengths and time available. If it doesn't make social media management a seamless part of running your business or takes too much time, you won't follow it for very long!

9.1. Design your sales and marketing funnel

Don't generate likes and followers from social media without a strategy for converting them into sales. This is where designing a step-by-step sales and marketing funnel becomes essential. You will need to understand what the steps are for ever so gently transforming your leads into paying clients and customers.

- Step 1: Attract - How do you get found?
- Step 2: Engage - How do you capture leads?
- Step 3: Nurture - How do you build relationships with your leads?
- Step 4: Sell - How do you turn them into customers?
- Step 5: Deliver – How do you provide excellent customer service so that your customers are happy to recommend you to others?

The most successful online marketers use social media as their lead generator and their email list as a sales generator.

Depending on the type of business you have, selling on social media may not work that well but social media is great for spreading the word and generating leads.

The key to making money from your social media marketing is to have an opt-in page on your website with an irresistible offer – and to use social media to drive traffic to it!

You can then continue building your relationship with your new leads by emailing them regularly with valuable and helpful content that builds relationships and trust and from time-to-time to sell your products and services with special offers!

After you have designed your funnel, you can streamline, systemise and automate it using an email marketing system so that it runs on autopilot and keeps bringing in a steady stream of leads while you are doing other things in your business!

10. Automated marketing system and online marketing and sales funnel

Once you are clear on your core message, ideal clients and content marketing plan you are allowed to start selecting your social media platforms! Well, at least when you are working with me you are!

Your automated marketing system will depend on:

- your goals and objectives
- what you are selling
- your best social media platform(s) based on your ideal clients
- your resources and strengths
- what is fun for you
- what kind of content you love creating or can easily create

10.1. What are social media tools?

We've been using the term 'social media' throughout this book, but what exactly does it mean and what makes it different from traditional media?

Think of regular media like newspapers, television and radio as a one-way street where you can receive information, but your ability to give feedback or interact is very limited.

Social media, on the other hand, is a two-way street where you can comment on and rate what you read or watch, start conversations and publish your own content.

In other words, social media sites are web sites that don't just give you information (one-way street), but also allow you to interact (two-way street) with the content provided on the web site.

Some of the most popular types of social media websites are:

- Social Bookmarking. (including Del.icio.us, StumbleUpon) These create interaction by allowing people to tag websites and search through websites bookmarked by other people.

- Social News. (including Digg, reddit) These create interaction by allowing people to vote for articles and comment on them.

- Social Networking. (including Facebook, Twitter, LinkedIn) These create interaction by allowing people to add friends, follow people or organisations, comment on posts, join groups and have discussions.

- Social Photo and Video Sharing. (including YouTube, Flickr, Instagram, Pinterest) These create interaction by allowing people to share photos or videos and comment on user submissions.

- Wikis. (including Wikipedia, Wikia) These create interaction with contributors who add articles and edit existing articles.

These websites are not the only social media websites. Any website that invites you to interact with the site and with other visitors falls under the definition of social media.

10.2. Popular social media tools

Blogs

- Blogs are websites or web pages that have built in functionality for posting, categorising and commenting on articles
- Blogs feature articles written by you. You are the expert and you can share your expertise with the world
- Blogs add fresh searchable content to websites that can be optimised for search engines
- Blogs can be videos if you are not a writer
- Blogs belong to you and your website and they won't go anywhere or change like other 3rd party social media tools

Facebook

- Social networking
- Millions of websites have integrated with Facebook
- Facebook business pages can include custom tabs, calls-to-action, videos and lead capture offers, shopping carts, etc.

Twitter

- Micro-blogging site in 140 characters
- Tweets can include an image
- The Twitter search engine gets 1 billion queries daily (probably even more by now…?)

Instagram

- Online photo and video sharing social network
- Allows users to share through a series of pictures

Google+

- Owned by Google and favoured in the Google search results
- Shows map locations in Google search results for local businesses
- Offers google hangouts platform for online meetings and webinars

YouTube

- Online video made by users
- Online video accounts for more than 60% of internet traffic
- YouTube is the second largest search engine

- The YouTube player is embedded across tens of millions of websites

LinkedIn

- Social networking site for the business community
- 97.3% of LinkedIn members use it for recruitment
- The largest B2B (business-to-business) networking site
- The average CEO has 930 connections on LinkedIn

Pinterest

- An online pinboard
- Beautiful visual interface – digital photo collages
- Users can set up pinboards for pinning photos
- Photos can be repinned, liked and commented upon

Socially optimised websites

- Have responsive designs – meaning they can be viewed across multiple devices including laptops, mobiles and tablets
- Include a blog for creating value-adding content for target audiences

- Show most common social sharing buttons to encourage sharing of articles and quotes on social media
- Can display dynamic content from social media profiles, including newsfeeds, posts and images from Facebook, videos from YouTube etc.

10.3. Select, set up, optimise, streamline, systemise, automate & go!

Integration, optimisation, systemisation and automation is the key to setting up efficient social media channels!

Why? It saves time and effort and builds momentum!

Many businesses focus on getting their branding and message right (which is great!) and might even have a high-level strategy in place, but automation is the step that is often missed and it is the last step that makes all the difference to your online marketing. It saves a ton of your time!

It is essential to select, setup, optimise, streamline, systemise and automate your online and social media marketing to save time and create more freedom in your life to do more of those things that you love!

Six steps to create your automated marketing system:

1. Select – those platforms your ideal clients are using

2. Set up – your social channels in a way that highlights your branding and core message so that your ideal clients can feel a connection with what you offer

3. Optimise – for people and search engines, but always for people first. Ensure your copy is professionally written to build connections and trust, but also include your keywords for search engine optimisation. And no, your best keywords may not be what you think they are, so it is best to conduct comprehensive keyword research regularly, if necessary using someone who speaks Google!

4. Streamline – integrate your social media platforms to make it easier to post and share.

5. Systemise – create your own social media management system and business processes that provide just the right amount of valuable content to your social platforms but only take up a reasonable amount of time. Most importantly,

have a plan so it is easy to spot opportunities for content that aligns with your brand.

6.   Automate - use social media management tools to monitor your platforms and schedule content delivery to multiple platforms at once to save time!

10.4. Getting help with social media management

We often say that there are three types of social media management tasks:

1) Fun tasks!

2) The ones you don't like!

3) The ones you don't have time for!

It is the tasks two and three that can become an obstacle, because if they are not fun, they rarely get done!

Here the old 80/20 rule becomes handy.

> 1. Focus on the 20% of tasks that are vital for your marketing, for the rest....
>
> 2. Delegate
>
> 3. Outsource
>
> 4. Automate
>
> 5. Eliminate

Social media marketing tasks that can be easily outsourced include:

- Online research for engaging and eye-catching images for your social media and blog posts
- Research for your social media content or blog posts
- Writing blog posts
- Publishing blog posts
- Distributing blog post links
- Posting and scheduling social media status updates
- Sharing your social media posts to multiple social media platforms (Twitter, Google+, LinkedIn)
- Uploading and keyword optimising your videos on YouTube and other video sharing sites
- Managing your LinkedIn profile
- Creating new lists in your email marketing system and uploading contacts and segmenting your database
- Creating and scheduling emails and auto-responders
- Creating email newsletters
- Keyword research for blog content
- EBook content research
- Simple EBook layout and formatting

11. Over to YOU

Now it's over to YOU. It's time to put those big plans into action. Jump in, get uncomfortable and shine your light! Your tribe is waiting for you to show up! And you'll thank yourself this time next year!

I'd love to hear your thoughts, questions and insights, please stay in touch!

Minna

minna@socialmediatribe.com.au

Find all links to my social media profiles on our website at

www.socialmediatribe.com.au

Looking forward to connecting with you there!

About the Author

Minna Salmesvuo

Social Media Marketing Strategist

Minna (MSc. Computer Information Systems – Commerce)
University of Jyvaskyla, Finland) has an 18-year
background as a business analyst and IT professional
implementing web-based business and marketing
solutions for clients in various industries including printing,

software development, manufacturing, higher education, professional services and retail.

Minna started Social Media Tribe in March 2011 to combine her passions (small business and marketing) and to provide online and social media marketing solutions to small business clients.

Minna specialises in social media strategy, core message and social media marketing tools automation using a strategic approach that integrates social media as a seamless part of everyday business and builds long-term relationships with target audiences.

Social Media Tribe

Empowering you to share your message with the world!

Based in Drysdale, Geelong, Australia, Social Media Tribe has implemented social media marketing solutions for clients in Melbourne, Geelong and Bellarine Peninsula since early 2011.

In 2015 we started offering Skype consulting sessions and this has allowed us to assist clients nationally and internationally. Some of our recent referral clients come from country Victoria, the Sydney area and North America!

At Social Media Tribe, we show small businesses how to get the most out of their social media marketing using a strategic approach that ensures their social media marketing campaign is aligned with their business goals, branding and resources. We create your strategy with you, set up and optimise your social media channels for efficiency and show you how to streamline, systemise and automate your social media management, lead generation and sales conversion.

www.socialmediatribe.com.au

www.ingramcontent.com/pod-product-compliance
Lightning Source LLC
Chambersburg PA
CBHW061610220326
41598CB00024BC/3523